Ordinary to Extraordinary

Also by Tabatha DeBruyn:

Creating Joy and Success Through Social Marketing

Ordinary to Extraordinary

An Inspired Guide to Living the Life of Your Dreams

Tabatha DeBruyn

Creating Life By Design

KITCHENER, ONTARIO, CANADA

Creating Life by Design
Kitchener, Ontario, Canada
www.CreatingLifeByDesign.net

Book Layout © 2017 BookDesignTemplates.com
Copy Editing by Stephanie Gunning
Cover design by Alejandra Blanco and Gus Yoo

Ordinary to Extraordinary/ Tabatha DeBruyn. —1st ed.
ISBN 978-0-9909574-0-9

To Shawn, Justin, and Jordan, and all my mentors, who have ignited my desire to serve. I want to deeply honour the works of the many authors who have come before me and all who have influenced my thought patterns and subconscious programming. I appreciate all you have shared with me, and it is my sincere desire that by using my own self-expression these philosophies will continue to empower more individuals to live life aligned with their highest selves.

Contents

Acknowledgments

IT IS WITH LOVE AND GRATITUDE that I acknowledge the family, friends, and many mentors who encourage me to tap into my true potential. Your ongoing support gives me the courage and the curiosity to continue to step out of my comfort zone and into a life of tremendous adventure, expanded love, and greater contribution. Thank you.

I would like to extend my sincere appreciation to Stephanie Gunning, my editor and cheerleader. I'm grateful for your passion for the content, your ongoing support, and your ability to weave words in perfect alignment with what my heart desires to express.

Thank you to both Alejandra Blanco and Gus Yoo for your help in designing the cover.

I am grateful to my husband, Shawn, and my boys, Justin and Jordan. You are my greatest teachers, and I learn from each of you every day. Your unwavering belief in me and your unconditional love have given me the grace to make mistakes, the space to grow, and the opportunity to take our lives from ordinary to extraordinary. I am grateful for the memories we've already created and feel incredibly eager and excited for the evolution and expansions that are yet to come.

Your Power & Potential Are Beyond Your Imagination

I'M THRILLED THAT YOU'VE PICKED UP **this book because it means you're ready to embrace how freak'n' amazing you are. You may not see it yet, or more importantly feel it, but you are powerful beyond your imagination, and the fact that you're reading this book means that you're ready to embrace this as your true current reality.**

I am writing this book from a loving, knowledgeable, relatable place to help you realize, or remember, that you are at your most spectacular when you stand firmly in 100 per cent self-expression and live as a confident individual in the midst of a shared human existence. At your core, you are perfect. This is the truth. You are an original expression of infinite potential with endless possibilities, and your authentic self-expression is needed right now. You are valuable and deserving.

Our world is filled with conformists, people who settle for doing and having much less than they are capable of creating. You are here to make a difference, here to help raise the consciousness of the world and to leave an incredible footprint. My intention in this book is to increase your awareness, give you tools, and hold unconditionally loving space for you so that you may shift from a fear-based, ego-screaming style of thought to an inspired, heart-based, ego-quieting knowing.

My message is intended for sleeping souls who are dying inside because they know they were destined to live a bigger life but need help to find their paths. If you are one of them, it's time for you to listen to the call to wake up and be uncaged. Set yourself free to express all your potential and power. The possibilities of what you can achieve are limitless.

In the pages of this book, I will give you the skills to build your confidence so you may experience joy, passion, and exquisite inner harmony. When you assimilate the information I am offering, you will be moved to frolic in your ability to self-love and create a magic-carpet-ride life rather than continue to live in fear, mediocrity, and distraction. You will learn to take 100 per cent responsibility, without judgment, for the life that has unfolded thus far, viewing it as perfect and filled with gifts and lessons. It is time to be grateful for the gifts, stop playing the victim, and start living an empowered, extraordinary life.

What makes me a self-mastery mentor with the ability to help people unlock the power they have within so they can begin living a life of joy and great abundance? Well, I have done it! I'm still very much a work in progress, but I have realized that playing small, hiding in the shadows and behind the theories of others is unacceptable. I no longer look for validation outside myself. Trying to feel significant to others would be to live gripped by fear. Fear is not my truth. I recognize that the fear I feel is a byproduct of the things

When you assimilate the information
I am offering, you will be moved to frolic in
your ability to self-love and create a magic-
carpet-ride life rather than continue to live
in fear, mediocrity, and distraction.

I thought about over and over until they became my known reality.

For much of my life, my brain was programmed to prove that these types of joy-squashing beliefs were my truth. I had created a life oriented around survival, following the herd and fitting in, thinking that this was the "right thing to do." I was not thriving. I was not living life with honest excitement and originality, or the energy of love. I was living life inflicted by *shoulds* and *not enoughness*. I had forgotten that I AM the creator of my life and that life is meant to be amazing.

For most of my life, I listened to the voices of well-meaning, loving people and influencers around me who told me what was right and what was wrong. These people I trusted told me what I should do and should not do, what I was good at and not good at, and more. I gave my power to everyone around me and stopped listening to my inner voice of knowing.

I now understand that what I learned as a young person led me to embrace a very narrow perception of reality. What my insecure self heard and discerned from parents, teachers, friends, naysayers, and bullies became my blueprint for life. My false understanding of what was possible and appropriate for me created some huge limiting factors in my day to day life as an adult. When you live that way long enough, you can live believing that your limitations are your destiny.

I was a queen chameleon. I learned to morph expertly into whatever kind of person would please others in the same situation. I wanted to be liked, appreciated, valued, significant, secure, and loved. What I did not know was that having all those feelings is an inside job. I looked outside myself for experiences that would give them to me. Because I gave my power away, my joy was at the mercy of other people. I was told to go to school, get good grades, get involved, work hard, find a career path, go to university, find a secure job, and that it would be even better if I had benefits and a pension. So, that's what I did. I got a double degree at a prestigious university, graduating with honours from a specialized program in education. I wasn't that smart; I just worked my ass off. Then I served as a high school teacher for fifteen years.

I enjoyed my time teaching and empowering teenagers to see their greatness, all the while understanding that I had not unlocked my own. I barely knew who Tabatha was and what made her happy. I was on the proverbial hamster wheel of life. I was a human *doer*, not a human *being*. I gave my calendar over to what was important to others and convinced myself that doing so made me an excellent human being of significance.

Meanwhile, a very quiet, yet persistent voice inside me kept nudging me to live a bigger life, one of choice, inspiration, and service on a larger scale. Funny how your path unfolds before you when you are ready, even if you don't understand or appreciate it at the time. Life can lead you to just the right knowledge, mentors, and possibilities if you are ready to notice them and you can muster up the courage to take action.

About seven years ago, I fell down a set of stairs, breaking my tailbone and fracturing several bones in my sacrum. My medical doctors recommended pain-killers and surgery, but my heart told me to heal differently. I aligned with a spiritual mentor who helped me understand that this event had happened *for* me, rather than *to* me. The injury to my physical body was in perfect alignment with the needs of my inner life because at that point I was ready to stand straight in my authentic power.

Within two weeks of my realization, I made a full recovery. None of the medical doctors I spoke with understood or could explain. My awareness of new possibilities, greater consciousness, and curiosity grew after that. And my desire for more authenticity, choice, and expansion in my life opened the doors of entrepreneurship to me. Within a year, I had built a multimillion-dollar business online, alongside my teaching career.

I am living proof that when you step boldly into your authentic power and align with your truth and your joy, magic happens. Today, after having stepped into my power, I have created a life of great contribution and financial wealth, I have traveled the world and had extraordinary adventures with inspiring people. But what I am most grateful for is the person I have become and the inner harmony I have found.

I have fallen in love with my far from perfect self—so much so that I now see that even my personal imperfections are perfect. My mistakes and detours have gifted me with lessons of true empathy, understanding, and compassion for others. I have learned what motivates me and what holds me back, and the process of self-discovery I have undergone has allowed me to become a tremendous success coach for others.

Today I serve the world as an inner harmony expert, a wealth coach, and a spiritual facilitator. Whatever name you want to give to what I do is up to you, but what I truly do is introduce people to their very best selves. I help people remember unconditional love for self so they may stand confidently and joyfully in the power of their self-expression.

Those who pick up this book are aligned and ready to engage in some deep self-discovery. You are ready to be reintroduced to the truth of the powerful self you have inside. You have a palpable desire to serve the world in a profound way. You are ready to unearth subconscious beliefs and programming that no longer serve you and to create an empowered and extraordinary life that you love.

I teach people how to move from settling to thriving, from ordinary to extraordinary. When you fall in love with the uniqueness of who you are and act from your 100 percent self-expression, you live from a state of grace that reveals choice and opportunities beyond your wildest imagination.

I am honoured to walk alongside you and be a mirror of your greatness until you own the profound power you have within. *Namaste.*

The best of me honours the best in you.

CHAPTER 1

The Battle Within

LET'S GET DOWN AND DIRTY. **And while we do, remember that rolling up your sleeves and digging in the dirt to get rid of the weeds makes room for new sprouts to grow. One day soon, these will create an incredible harvest.**

The fact that you have picked up a book such as this is a good indication that you want some part of your life to change for the better, even if only on a subconscious level. You know you are destined for more. There is at least a flicker of excitement in your mind when you consider the possibility of what lies before you.

I am here to guide you to understand that you have the capacity to create as much joy as you wish. This book

will give you the tools to make it happen step by step. With these tools, you can move from a stagnant life of quiet desperation to a life of making constant progress toward your dreams.

Before we get started, I ask you to take a moment, no matter how much knowledge, wisdom, success, and life experience you bring to your reading, to make sure your cup has room for more. If your mental cup is too full to accept something new, you may miss out on the slightly different perspective I am offering in these pages that can unlock the combination needed to reveal beauty to you beyond your current imagination. Remember, nature abhors a vacuum. If you leave space for new information that serves your highest self, wisdom will drop in and expand your consciousness.

Ask yourself: *Am I truly open to what this material has to offer?* If so, continue reading. If not, ask yourself: *Why am I resisting further expansion? Is my ego holding me back from exploring new possibilities?*

My intention for this workbook is that it allows you to develop a greater sense of self-love, inner harmony, and knowing that you can have all the delicious feelings you desire.

Once staying where you are becomes more painful to you than taking action to make progress, you will open the doors to a different reality.

To find the courage, self-discipline, and insights necessary to take bold action and create a different reality, it is important to take an honest look at where you are now. Once staying where you are becomes more painful to you than taking action to make progress, you will open the doors to a different reality. Doing so will give you great pleasure.

Do you feel unfulfilled in certain areas of your life?

Whoa, before you close this book because discomfort has crept in, pause for a moment. I get it! I know why it's hard even to ask the question.

Often it is easier to listen to our mind chatters and defensively justify where we are than it is to look honestly and objectively at our lives. Some of us love telling our stories of unfulfilled potential because the roles we

The key is to realize that up until this point everything has unfolded in perfect order because it allowed you to become the person you are today.

play and the reasons why we are where we are have become our identity. Taking inventory of our lives often brings to the surface all kinds of learned limitations—crap thinking. All the lowest vibration feelings, such as shame, guilt, blame, not enoughness, and *blah blah blah* arise. I know it all too well because I swam in that pool of egoic self-sabotaging yuck for years as I was contemplating making changes in my life.

Having reached the other side of the pool, I'm here to tell you that taking a good look at where you are and at the gap between here and where you want to be doesn't have to be uncomfortable. The key is to realize that up until this point everything has unfolded in perfect order because it allowed you to become the person you are today. There is no need for judgment. In fact, just know that feeling the contrast of the rain and the sun makes your appreciation when you feel the warmth of the sun or the moist coolness of the rain much greater.

As you move forward, the only thing that matters is this moment right here. This moment is all you ever have. Your past is gone, and you are creating your future. Your energy vibration and current thoughts will determine what you attract and experience moving forward. Of course, your past matters and you must take 100 per cent responsibility for where you are right now, but not heavy, self-incriminating responsibility.

I want to lighten things up and lead you to the magic of making 100 per cent conscious responses with your actions moving forward because you do have the ability to respond consciously. When you do this, you will no longer be a victim of your circumstances. Rather you will be a warrior and a magician at creating your current reality.

It is freeing to relinquish control over what happens to you and to realize that you only have control over how you respond. You respond to life through the energy, thoughts, and inspired actions you put out in every moment.

"When I began working with Tabatha's tools, I felt so stuck! Stuck in my business, my relationship, and emotionally. Within one session, I began to unravel what had been tangled up for decades."

—SHANNON CROWDER, AGE 42,
HOLISTIC LIFE MENTOR AND ENTREPRENEUR

Your previous actions, thoughts, and associations brought you into alignment with this book. To me, this signifies that you are ready to move from where you are to a new level of conscious understanding. This change of state is needed because we cannot solve problems in the same state we create them. You are ready to acknowledge and ignite the potential within you to create a different reality. Knowledge is power, and you are ready to receive and remember the truth that you are the creator of everything in your life, which is meant to be amazing. In fact, your number one responsibility is to do whatever you can to feel wonderful at this moment. Once you know this information, you can't "unring" the bell, and you will craft your life from a new place of understanding, excitement, and empowerment.

> This change of state is needed because we cannot solve problems in the same state we create them.

Before coming to these realizations for myself, I was in the constant cycle of self-fulfilling prophecy. The longer I dwelled in the energy of mediocrity, the more steadfast I was about staying put in my "fine" life. One of our human needs is for security, and if we live our lives a certain way long enough, we begin to settle into the groove of thinking that being where we are is all that we are capable of and deserve.

The ego is powerful. As our sense of identity, it is motivated to keep us safe. Whether it truly continues to serve us or not, it keeps us from exploring unknown territory.

As the years went by, the chatter in my mind justifying why staying where I was in each area of my life was the best and safest course for me became even more clever and convincing. My ego became so strong that I was paralyzed and felt I couldn't act to create any type of change.

The thoughts we have over and over become our beliefs. A belief is simply a practised thought. Your mind will try to find evidence to prove your beliefs are true to you. Your beliefs are what motivate you to take action—or in my case, not to take action.

Every time I thought about an area of my life expanding into more joy, my mind chatter would chime in to prevent it. If you could hear a recording of the battling thoughts of my true self, nudging me toward expansion, and the thoughts of my ego, attempting to squash me into a box of scarcity, you would hear a remark that sounds something like the following.

Tab's ego: "You have way more than most, how dare you lust after more? You're so greedy, materialistic, ungrateful, and 'high maintenance.' Your life is just fine."

When an exciting desire bubbled up in me, my ego would squash it much like a version of the arcade game Whack-a-Mole. My true self would have a desire and Tab's ego would smack it on the head and push it right back down.

> The thoughts we have over and over become our beliefs.

Here's another example. I would start thinking about how amazing it would be to have more money so my husband and I could travel with our kids and let them learn about the diversity of the world and different cultures. Tab's ego would pipe in with: "You don't need more money. You have lots of food to eat where you are. Spending money on travel is not necessary. Have you watched the news lately? You should simply be grateful for the food you have."

Well, today I realize that none of what my ego shared was remotely relevant because I have always been grateful for the food I have. I have never taken the good in my life for granted. What has wanting more money to flow into my life so I can travel with my children to do with the fact that I have food in my belly? Nothing!

After a while, I was in a pattern of feeling guilt, shame, and helplessness whenever I thought of traveling with my kids. My entire body felt them energetically. These constricting feelings kept me from creating a different reality.

We unconsciously give great power over to the limited sense of identity of our egos. Now I know that a feeling of constriction in my body is never the truth but only rather a reaction to something I have heard or seen or thought. But I didn't know this back then.

What other craziness would you hear from Tab's self-limiting ego? "You should be grateful to have a husband who loves and respects you. How dare you long to have massive physical attraction, growing mental stimulation, and passion with him?"

My thoughts often went to a place of believing I did not deserve, and it even was not possible to create the kind of incredible relationship I desired.

Did you know that your thoughts become your reality? This assertion is not just "new-age fluff," it is neuroscience. Your brain operates in different modes. Your conscious mental activity uses about 5 per cent of your brain power. Your unconscious mental activity uses approximately 95 per cent of your brain power.

Your brain has an incredible component called the *reticular activating system* (RAS), which acts as a filter between your conscious mind and your unconscious mind. Your conscious mind can take in about forty bits of data in a second, whereas your unconscious mind can take in millions of bits of data in a second.

Can you imagine what would happen if you tried to process that volume of information consciously? You would go crazy. Your RAS allows only the important stuff to filter through to your conscious mind to process. But—and this is the important part—how does it determine what is and is not important? It knows because you tell it.

Your RAS acts as a filter between your conscious and unconscious minds.

What you focus on most of the time determines what is important for your **RAS** system to share with you. Have you ever noticed that once you decide there is a certain car you want you begin seeing them everywhere? That's because your **RAS** now knows this car is important so it signals you to take note.

Eight years ago, my thoughts were such that it was impossible to have respect, passion, and continuous growth in a relationship and my brain proved this to me all day long. I saw divorce, unhappiness, affairs, and people settling for mediocrity all around me. Seeing this, I felt so paralyzed with fear that I could not take steps to create something different. I was out of integrity because deep down I wanted more.

Did you know that you can have both respect and passion in a marriage? They are not exclusive. That's likely what both parties in every couple want, and if you have the desire, it is not too much to ask for and create.

Your desires are the nudges of your inner self to fulfill your human needs for variety and continuous growth and expansion. Without variety and growth, we live lives that lack happiness and fulfillment.

You can live in a state of absolute bliss and contentment accompanied by eager excitement and high motivation to anticipate and imagine what's to come.

When it comes to my body image, Tab's ego would pipe in with: "Your body is healthy and supports all your daily activity, so why does it matter that it's not lean and muscular? You are fine! You have just looked at too many fitness ads on social media and you have unrealistic expectations."

By listening to my ego's chatter, I programmed my RAS to create comfort with my then-current state. I did not challenge myself to create what I desired, which was greater health and vitality. Instead, I became a woman who would not draw attention to herself.

Staying in your comfort zone denies you of fulfilling your need for continuous growth. Giving up the comfort zone does not mean that you must live in a place that lacks contentment. It means the opposite. You can live in a state of absolute bliss and contentment accompanied by eager excitement and high motivation to anticipate and imagine what's to come.

If we were to dissect further the dialogue between my inner self, which wanted to expand, and Tab's ego, you would hear: "You have a steady paycheque coming in, so you don't always need to be creative and try new things or touch more people." My RAS system was programmed to keep me right where I was, rather than move me to where I desired to be.

We spend most of our waking hours in our jobs, and if we are not fully expressing ourselves during those hours of our lives and expanding our talents and skills, we need to rethink how we are spending our time.

Even though there were big gaps of logic in the advice from my ego, at the time I did not have enough awareness to recognize that the conclusions I was coming to, were ridiculous and immensely self-limiting. I was settling for mediocrity, sleepwalking through life, and maintaining the status quo—staying small. I needed to wake up, stop the insanity, quiet my ego, and start listening to my inner knowing and emotional guidance system. I needed to decide that enough was enough because the reality was that I was not feeling progress, expansion, and joy. I had become a victim of my own life. I was no longer the writer of my story. I had given away so much of my power that I was now living in a cesspool of unfulfilled potential.

Fortunately, deep down I knew I was destined for more.

CHAPTER 2

Take Inventory with Detached Observation

MY GUESS IS THAT YOU ARE READY **to wake up and start transforming your life for the better. Ready to move from the shadows into your magnificent light. In this chapter, I will ask you to take an honest look at the level of joy you have in all areas of your life.**

Are you able to meet your human need for security?

Do you have a fulfilling level of variety in your life?

Do you wake up with purpose and passion for the day ahead, knowing that you are living a life of significance?

Are your connections with others authentic and meaningful?

Are you continuing to grow and expand into your full potential?

Are you contributing to a purpose beyond yourself?

Think of your health, your wealth, your relationships, your spirituality, your level of contribution and significance. Are they at the level you truly wish them to be?

Where do you see unfulfilled potential?

How does your current life look?

Below, describe five areas of your life in which you see the potential for improvement.

1._____

_____

_____

2._____

_____

_____

3._____

_____

_____

4._____

_____

_____

5._____

_____

_____

Here is where we draw the line between the A players and the B players. A players are those who are ready to actively change their lives. B players are those who are passively contemplating the idea of making changes. These are the people who often say: "I know..." but then don't do anything to make things better. Many people say they want to create change, but only a few decide to make it happen.

Life is like an adventure novel in which you get to choose your adventure. You get to decide the outcome toward which you are working. If you sincerely want to transform your life, you must apply the tools available to you, engage in study to improve your skills and acquire knowledge, and actively participate. If you have not acknowledged and written down the areas of your life you want to see improved yet, I encourage you to trust in the process and go back to do so now.

If you sincerely want to transform your life, you must apply the tools available to you, engage in study to improve your skills and acquire knowledge, and actively participate.

Listen to your inner knowing. Be honest with yourself. Which areas of your life don't bring you great joy yet? Taking the step of naming these areas will give you the ability to play actively with the possibility of creating something different for yourself.

If you're hearing a lot of mind chatter, I encourage you to tame your ego because right now it feels threatened. Put pen to paper and remember this: Making an honest assessment is not looking at your past and judging it a failure, rather it is seeing that all you have been through has created the stepping stones needed to follow a new pathway to greater joy and fulfillment.

You can trust that "with faith as small as a mustard seed, you can move mountains. Nothing is impossible for you" (Matthew 17:20).

When you have written down the areas of your life that you know you want to change, I ask you to celebrate the fact that you have new awareness. Awareness is the first step, and it's a big one! You quieted the ego long enough to respect and honour your inner knowing.

"Tabatha has helped me find acceptance and alignment within myself. Her compassionate teachings have allowed me to discover true happiness and inspired me to live my best life. This has given me peace."

—KAITLYN FIELD, AGE 24,
STUDENT AND ENTREPRENEUR

Listen carefully to inspiration because it is powerful beyond belief. Likely, you also have an ego playing tricks with you, so let my hindsight be your foresight. Thank any second-guessing thoughts that you've had for their contribution, but see these limiting ideas with lightness and a bit of laughter when you consider how your ego just doesn't know better. Your ego is working from the blueprint of your much younger self, whereas your desire for more comes from the essence of who you are, a wiser part of you that knows what is possible yet has not yet been realized. Listen to this voice and understand that from internal inspiration comes new progression, expansion, and joy.

Feeling joyful, harmonious, and significant is your birthright. You were born with infinite potential. You are the creator of your human experience. You have free will to create whatever level of fulfillment you desire. You need to decide right now that the pain of staying as you are is greater than the discomfort of change. As Robin Sharma, a mentor of mine, often shares, change is always terribly uncomfortable in the beginning and super messy in the middle, but it's magnificent on the other side.

You will want to turn back to your norm. It's human nature to go back to what is comfortable. I can prove it to you with a simple exercise.

Hold your hands in front of you.

Interlace the fingers of both hands with your thumbs one on top of the other the way you usually do.

Now, switch your thumbs, so the opposite one is on top. This is extremely uncomfortable, isn't it? The brain wants to signal the thumbs to go back to their original positions.

> Listen to this voice and understand that from internal inspiration comes new progression, expansion, and joy.

We are creatures of habit. For this reason, it takes determination, a decided heart, and some grit to move from where you are to where you desire to be. To help solidify your conviction to transform each of these areas of your life, I ask you now to look at the consequences you will face if you keep doing what you are doing in five years' time. I want you to begin to realize that being as you are today is no longer comfortable. If you stay where you are in any of these areas you will be out of integrity.

Generally, when you have a desire, it means that you are not fully self-expressed or living up to your 100 percent true potential. Being out of integrity means you are living less than whole, so your feelings will continue to remind you that something is out of alignment.

Below, write down all the negative outcomes that you imagine will or could become your reality if you choose not to change.

Write using the same five areas of your life as you did in the first exercise. Consequences in five years' time, if you continue   living the way you are include:

1._____

_____

_____

_____

_____

2._____

_____

_____

_____

_____

3._____

_____

_____

_____

_____

4._____

_____

_____

_____

_____

5._____

_____

_____

_____

_____

Take a moment to feel into each of these consequences. The experience of imagining the feeling of
pain and constriction from staying the same as you are
today will help you take your head out of the sand and
truly decide that you're ready to change. In fact, you

want to feel so much mental resolve about your decision to change that you feel like saying: "How dare I not change?" You want to feel that it is a crime to continue living with unfulfilled potential.

You are the creator of your life. Are you ready for change? Are you ready to trade your ordinary in for extraordinary? If the answer to these questions is yes, let's get started because this is the first day of the rest of your life!

CHAPTER 3

Raise Your Energy Frequency

IN CHAPTER 2, I ASKED YOU TO LOOK **at your areas of unfulfilled potential and imagine what would happen if you continued down the same road for the next five years. I know that's not a particularly fun thing to do, but I am proud of you for having the courage to look at what you have created up until now.**

I am also proud of you for taking responsibility for what you are creating from this moment forward. You are ready to release what no longer

serves your highest self and to tap into the energy that creates infinite possibilities.

Taking an honest look at your unfulfilled potential likely has tied your stomach in knots and sent your emotions into overdrive. These sensations are often not pleasant, but it is necessary to feel them because from emotion comes the desire to be in motion. In fact, your emotions are your greatest guidance system.

If you are not feeling good and your goal is to live a life of joy and productivity, your most important next action is to find a way to feel better.

Every emotion we feel produces a biochemical reaction in the body. Therefore, they are vibrational indicators of what to do. If you are not feeling good and your goal is to live a life of joy and productivity, your most important next action is to find a way to feel better.

Let me remind you again, when you are feeling less than joyful, there is no need to judge. Rather, be proud of your awareness. Celebrating awareness prevents negative thoughts and feelings from gaining momentum.

Contrasting what we don't want in life with what we do want in life gives us great clarity. Sometimes we are motivated to run away from something and other times we are motivated to run towards something. Both types of motivation create action. Your purpose is to focus your mind in ways that motivate you to take the action that will enable you to manifest your full potential.

"After a few sessions, I am living with passion—setting goals I didn't think were possible and achieving them! I competed in a body building competition, became part of a successful rock band, hiked in an active volcano, explored Mayan ruins, and met the love of my life."

—PHILIP HEASLIP, AGE 32,
PARAMEDIC AND MUSICIAN

I want you to look at where you are right now with great satisfaction because your past has made you who you are and propelled you to evolve. Your evolution has brought you to the place you are right now where you are ready to learn. Any fear you are feeling is simply a learned programme that no longer serves you. If you can turn this into gratitude, you can release it. You have gained valuable knowledge, incredible skills, and empathy for others from coping with your own difficulties. Be grateful for these lessons.

It is important not to look back at your life and dwell on feelings of blame, shame, guilt, or any other low-vibrational emotion. The easiest way to shift our energy when we feel these things is to practice gratitude. Your next step is to sift through your past experiences and find the gifts for which you can be grateful. If you doubt there is anything of value, do the exercise anyway. I have learned that you can find a treasure in a big, steamy pile of crap if you look closely.

This activity takes courage and maturity and a lot of unconditional love, but this process will transmute energy and allow you more ease when moving forward. Start with something small and then look for what else this situation gave you.

Take a look at the different areas of your life. What are you grateful for? Write down the gifts you identify. As you do, feel gratitude in your heart for what you have learned and the skills and stories you have gained. Discovering your gifts is an essential step in the journey from where you are to the inner harmony of knowing that you can and deserve to create a different future.

Look back at the five areas you indicated had the potential for improvement and find the gifts for which you are grateful.

1._____

_____

_____

_____

_____

2._____

_____

_____

_____

_____

3._____

_____

_____
_____
_____

4._____
_____
_____
_____
_____

5._____
_____
_____
_____
_____

When you live with an attitude of gratitude, you live in the energy that creates endless possibilities. The vibration of gratitude is in the higher end of the scale of frequencies, a level that feels expansive and draws wonderful opportunities to you.

When you live with an attitude of gratitude, you live in the energy that creates endless possibilities.

Vibration is simply a way of describing the energy that surrounds your overall state of being at any given time. It is like your energy signature, reflecting your inner most thoughts, feelings, and beliefs. If you are resistant to the idea of energy vibration, that's okay. The place of your greatest resistance is where your greatest growth can occur.

The law of attraction is the magnetic power of the universe that draws similar energies together. Thoughts, ideas, people, situations, and circumstances are forms of energy. You must act with clarity, purpose, and intention if you are to create the life you wish. The vibration of the energy you put out will attract similar energy patterns to you.

Because everything is made up of energy, if you want to change your life, you must change the vibration that surrounds you and within you. Feelings of gratitude are the fastest way to increase your vibration and actively put you on a path to more fulfillment and inner harmony.

The place of your greatest resistance is where your greatest growth can occur.

When consciously creating the life you wish to lead, it serves you to raise the frequency of your vibration. It is difficult to move from the common human frequencies of fear, doubt, and frustration to frequencies of love, joy, and peace; even so, moving up the energy scale is an important skill to master.

Sometimes changing your thoughts and how you feel can be extremely difficult. Here are twelve techniques that can help you to shift your vibration to match the positive feelings you wish to experience in life. In raising your vibration, you can optimize your ability to receive thoughts, ideas, people, situations, and circumstances, and increase the number and quality of the opportunities that come to you and the speed you can receive them. Becoming mindful of your thoughts and the way you feel is most important. When you change your thoughts, you will change your world. A lofty phrase but so true.

1. CHOOSE YOUR ASSOCIATIONS CAREFULLY. **You are a product of the people with whom you spend**

time. Have you ever noticed that when you spend time with people who eat mindfully and choose clean, low-calorie foods, you tend to make healthier choices yourself? Have you noticed that when you spend time with people who freely use profanity you find yourself swearing like a sailor? I know I often spend way more money when I go shopping with people who spend freely and don't pay attention to price tags than I do when I'm shopping with people on set budgets.

Becoming mindful of your thoughts and the way you feel, is most important.

It is important that you become mindful of those you allow to influence you. Spend time with people you feel good around. Spend time with people living the lifestyle you want. Spend time with people who support your growth. Limit your time with those who don't. And remember, it takes courage, compassion, and self-love to know you are worthy of spending your time with people who hold space for you to become your happiest self.

Positive influences don't all have to be people you've met in person. I spend a lot of time reading illuminating books and listening to uplifting podcasts. Setting boundaries and making choices to protect and expand my mindset is one of the greatest gifts I give myself.

2. SPEND TIME IN NATURE, IN LIGHT, AROUND COLOUR, AND IN WATER. **Next time you get in a funk, look for ways the four elements of earth, air, fire, and water can support you. Go out and spend time in nature and the sunlight, if possible. Light a candle and take in the comfort and clarity it provides. Appreciate the colours of the trees, the intricacies of the flowers, listen to the birds or the crunch of the snow beneath your feet, fill your lungs with fresh air. The energy field of untouched nature is at such a high frequency that your personal energy field transmutes in its presence.**

Having a bath or going swimming and being supported by the element of water can help raise your vibration. Even taking the time to wash your hands or consume water can help change your energy level.

3. TAKE TIME TO ENGAGE YOUR SENSES. **Look for, and appreciate pleasant sights, smells, tastes, sounds, and textures. We run at such a frenetic**

pace in society today that we often don't take time to savour and thoroughly enjoy the beauty of all that is around us. By slowing down to enjoy the sensation of putting your hands around a warm cup of fragrant tea in your favourite mug, you will change your energy vibration. As you will if you put on a piece of music that automatically causes your body to move.

By stopping, looking people in the eyes when they're speaking to you, and listening to understand them, rather than formulating your next thought, you can lift your vibration. To simply take the time to feel the fabric of your clothes and smell the freshness as you put on a recently laundered comfy sweatshirt can raise the frequency of your energy.

So, get out of your overthinking head and into the feelings in your body. By doing this, you stop the momentum of lower vibration energy and make space for a new frequency.

4. EXERCISE AND DO THINGS YOU LOVE. **Whether you love running, weight lifting, or having sex, getting your body moving and sending more oxygen to your cells will clear your mind and shift**

your energy. The coordination involved in doing any physical activity distracts you from your mind chatter and slows the momentum of negative energy. Exercise is an opportunity for a new, higher frequency of energy to get into your body.

5. EAT CLEANLY. **Everything is energy. When you choose to eat foods that have high levels of energy in them, you fuel your body with great energy. The closer to nature your food is, the higher the level of energy you can extract from it. Eating processed foods with many preservatives, by contrast, fuels your body with lower level energy.**

This said, if eating ice cream brings you great joy, you can gain high-level energy from it. But if eating that same ice cream causes you to judge yourself and feel guilty, don't eat it! How you feel is a great indicator as to the level of energetic frequency you can expect from your food.

6. PRACTISE RANDOM ACTS OF KINDNESS. **Helping people causes your body to release endorphins, serotonin, and dopamine which, as they are absorbed in your bloodstream raise your vibration.**

In fact, you will lift not only your own energy but also the energy of the recipients of your kindness as well as that of onlookers. Random acts of kindness have a powerful ripple effect. Much like tipping over a set of dominos, beautiful energy gets passed on—and passed on in ways the original giver could not imagine.

Try doing something nice for someone today that they would never expect and see how great you feel afterwards. Then watch as the law of attraction continues to put things in your path to keep you feeling that way.

7. MEDITATE. **Meditation is a valuable tool for managing your vibration because it simply quiets your thoughts. Through focusing on breathing diaphragmatically, it stops the momentum of negative energy and makes space for new frequencies to be experienced.**

You can never be in a state of fear and gratitude at the same time!

8. EXPRESS APPRECIATION AND PRACTICE FEELING GRATEFUL. **Gratitude can always lift your vibration. Active appreciation for even the smallest of**

things around you can make a huge difference in your energy field. You can never be in a state of fear and gratitude at the same time! Remember this the next time fear creeps in.

What do you see to be grateful for? You don't have to look far to revel in gratitude. The fact that you have eyes to read this book, hands to hold it, a chair to sit on, clean air to breathe, the brain power to understand and assimilate the information, the frame of reference to experience the material on a level that is just for you, and so on, are all reasons to be grateful.

By acknowledging your appreciation for everything you experience, you can increase your energetic vibration.

9. FIVE FEET FIVE MINUTES. **Sometimes simply removing myself from a situation and putting myself in a different environment is enough to shift my energy. When frustration hits, a little time away from the same people, problems, and environment allows me to get in touch with a new perspective and out of a frustrating energy state. Try this the next time you feel a discussion moving in a negative direction. Simply remove yourself for**

five minutes. Put yourself at least five feet away from your original physical space. As Dr. Wayne Dyer says: "When you change the way you look at things, often the things you look at change". When you come back to the original position, you can often see things and respond very differently in ways that serve all parties more positively.

10. CREATE A SAFE WORD. **Sometimes when negative energy picks up momentum, it becomes contagious and takes on a life of its own among those with whom you are close. This momentum can escalate so rapidly that you can have no awareness of the law of attraction at work. It's easy to get caught up in the momentum and then say things we don't mean and may regret. But if you have a safe word, it can jar everyone out of an intense discussion and bring them back to neutrality.**

In my household, populated by two teenage boys and two passionate parents, we use the word *marshmallow* as a safe word. If one of us realizes what is happening, we have agreed—no questions asked—that when *marshmallow* is said, we stop and come back to our truths. We take five minutes and move five feet, or take other measures to halt the negativity. Even in the heat of the moment, when one of us uses the safe word, everybody often ends up breaking out in laughter because we see how ridiculous it was that we were feeding off each other and how things got carried away.

11. LAUGHTER IS THE BEST MEDICINE. **If you can find a way to laugh, your energy state will immediately change. You can't be mad and laugh at the same time. Perhaps it's a comedian you have a link to on your phone, a memory that always makes you laugh, a person who always cracks you up, or a movie that makes you laugh every time. Whatever it is, use it. Laughter releases endorphins and distracts your mind from whatever thoughts are keeping you in a lower energy vibration.**

12. MAKE A LIST OF THINGS THAT MAKE YOU HAPPY. **I know this sounds a bit ridiculous. Sometimes getting out of a funk is harder for me than I'd like to admit. For such occasions, I find that having tools at my fingertips can help me incrementally move up the vibrational scale so I can even get to a place where I am at least open to getting off my butt, going out in nature, sitting down to meditate, or laughing.**

We humans can be stubborn creatures sometimes. We often choose to stay in our funks even though we feel terrible and know that changing vibration would be best for us. Therefore, I have a list of words stored in my phone that I can go to when I'm low. When I read these words out loud and feel into them, I always start to feel better.

That's all I'm ever going for: to feel better than I do right now.

I'm going to share my list, and I encourage you to make a similar list.

- Acceptance
- Amazing
- Beautiful
- Blessed
- Blissful
- Bold
- Brilliant
- Charming
- Confident
- Creative
- Curious
- Delicious
- Empowered
- Excellent
- Exquisite
- Fascinating
- Frisky
- Inspired
- Majestic
- Secure
- Seductive
- Sparkling

My husband and I have been together for twenty-five-plus years. On the rare occasions when my husband is driving me crazy, which happens, I made a list of a bunch of the things I love most about him, just in case I forget. Reading my list and remembering these things slows down the momentum of a negative energy and floods my body with good feelings and memories. It changes my state and brings in gratitude and a new perspective, which in turn shifts me to a higher vibration of energy.

At the end of this chapter, you will see a series of emotions which I've drawn from the Abraham-Hicks Emotional Guiding System. This list shows the relative vibrational levels of different emotions you may experience throughout the day. Your goal is not to feel the need to jump from very low to very high. Be patient. Moving up the scale takes time. We usually can't leap from feeling shame to joy. But using these tools can help us work up the scale.

The more emotional awareness and maturity we have by making it a priority to mind our energy field, the fewer lower vibrational energies we will attract and the faster we can move from a low level of energy to a higher one that better serves us.

Raising our energy comes with practice. The key is to develop the awareness of your energy level and use the tools that resonate with you most to raise your frequency higher. For example, if you are feeling angry, do your best to feel pride or courage and you will shift your vibration incrementally higher.

When you understand how the law of attraction works to create your reality, you will no doubt want to ensure that you do all you can so that your vibration matches the energy of that which you wish to create in your life.

EMOTIONAL SCALE

1. Joy/Appreciation/Empowered/
Freedom/Love
2. Passion
3. Enthusiasm/Eagerness/Happiness
4. Positive Expectation/Belief
5. Optimism
6. Hopefulness
7. Contentment
8. Boredom
9. Pessimism
10. Frustration/Irritation/Impatience
11. Overwhelment
12. Disappointment
13. Doubt
14. Worry
15. Blame
16. Discouragement
17. Anger
18. Revenge
19. Hatred/Rage
20. Jealousy
21. Insecurity/Guilt/Unworthiness
22. Fear/Grief/Depression/Despair/
Powerlessness

CHAPTER 4

How Do You Want to Feel?

NOW THAT YOU HAVE CLARITY **about the past and gratitude for all it has made of you, the page turns, and we can move on to the fun stuff!**

Let's look at what you desire and view its manifestation not as a struggle, but as a journey of passion and inspired action, knowing that it is meant to be yours. You understand that your current thoughts and feelings are of the utmost importance in this process. I want you to start to dream about each area of your life and think about how you want to feel.

The reason we desire something is that we believe it will make us feel better. When you look at each area of your life, what is it that you most want to create and what feelings will run through your body when you achieve them? You want to make these feelings crystal clear.

Here are some feelings to consider:

- Accepted
- Appreciated
- Balanced
- Confident
- Contented
- Desired
- Free
- Fulfilled
- Happy
- Joyful
- Loved
- Passionate
- Peaceful
- Prosperous
- Safe
- Satisfied
- Secure
- Significant
- Stable
- Successful
- Valued
- Worthy

Do not limit your desires to the words on this list. Rather, use this list as a starting point.

Remember, every desire you feel in your body and create in your imagination will attract like things to you. Other things will manifest to make you feel more of the same way. Thus, you are well on your journey to creation or manifestation of your dreams.

In each area of your life,
what do you want to feel?

Please notice that I did not ask "What goal do you have for each area of your life?" (I know this is an extremely uncomfortable question for all the "control freaks" who are my readers. I know, because I was one!)

Please suspend your disbelief and trust me as I take you further down the path to creating an extraordinary life. Suspending disbelief is important because the *how* is not in our control. The fact that we try to manipulate how things happen is silly considering that our perspective is limited. The universe has a bird's eye view— a much better view than ours—on all the different ways to align us with all we wish to achieve. If you try to control how things happen, you will be cutting off possibilities you may not be able to see right now. Of course, you need to take purposeful inspired, informed action to begin to feel how you want to feel, but you must also learn to surrender exactly how possibilities in your life will unfold.

Using the same five areas of your life as you have for the previous exercises, write down a list of how you would like to feel. This exercise will be more powerful if you keep working on the same goals.

1._____

_____

_____

_____

_____

2._____

_____

_____

_____

_____

3._____

_____

_____

_____

_____

4._____

_____

_____

_____

_____

5._____

_____

_____

_____

As you begin dreaming about how you want to feel, you will likely experience some self-doubt, criticizing thoughts, and skepticism. These are signs of your ego at work, trying to keep you where you are. The ego feels threatened because it only knows what you have experienced thus far. The unknown is new territory. As you are making notes about how you want to feel in each of these areas, attune to your body. This exercise is an opportunity to discern if what you are experiencing is true (something objectively factual), a learned programme, or a distorted belief that no longer serves you.

Now try something else. Think of a time when you felt complete elation, a time when you were so full of life that tears of joy nearly spill out of your eyeballs. When I think of my children belly laughing, I can feel each of the cells in my heart expand and I experience a deep inner happiness.

Identify and describe in detail a time when you have felt incredible expansion.

_____

_____

_____

_____

_____

_____

What exact sensations did you feel?

_____

_____

_____

_____

_____

_____

_____

When I think of one of my children's piercing scream of pain coming from the other room. I feel my breath become shallow, my heart nearly stops, and my cells constrict.

Identify a time when you felt excruciating constriction. Describe the situation in detail.

_____

_____

_____

_____

_____

_____

What exact sensations did you feel?

_____

_____

_____

_____

_____

_____

_____

I had you experience this exercise to attune you to how your body changes according to your thoughts. Your thoughts create a biochemical response in your body, much like the one that happens when you think of biting into a lemon. Imagine it, and your mouth begins to salivate. An eye may twitch just at thinking of the sour taste.

Now you have proof that your thoughts create feelings and your feelings change your vibration. The energy you put out is the energy you will attract.

The tricky part about minding our thoughts and our feelings is that we are highly motivated by our early childhood programming. Most of our subconscious programming occurs between from birth to age eight. Because we were so young when our parents, grandparents, teachers, religious mentors, and other childhood authority figures imposed this information on us, we did not have a frame of reference to decide what was true and what was false. Thus, our perception of the information we received was that it was true. Our early programming gave us our blueprints for life and taught us how to show up in the world, including how to love and be loved, and how to stay safe or take a risk.

"As a psychotherapist, I work with people swimming through dark waters. Tabatha's techniques help me retain my strength and maintain my health so that I do not sink."

—LISA MARIE MCGREAL, AGE 43,
SPIRITUAL PSYCHOTHERAPIST AND SOCIAL WORKER

In this book, I don't feel the need to take you back to each of the childhood events that installed your programming, but I do need you to become aware of what is the factual truth and what is learned. An important truth is that you came here as a perfect extension of infinite potential and unconditional love. You did not arrive as a baby thinking: "I am not worthy," "I am flawed," "I'm not good with money," "I am destined to be overweight," or "I'll be abandoned." You had these and many other beliefs imposed on you, somehow or another. Because we continue to think such ideas repeatedly over years they become our truths and our beliefs. Beliefs motivate our actions and our reactions.

As you wrote down your desires, did you notice what your body was feeling? Did any thoughts arise that caused your muscles to contract? These contractions show you the beliefs you had learned as a child that no longer serve you.

Note the presence of any thoughts telling you why what you want is impossible or why you don't deserve it, but don't agree with them or give them your power. Remember, these are the old programmes that have kept you where you are.

Let's do another exercise. For this one, I want you to read the five descriptions you wrote only moments ago of feelings you would like to have when attaining one of your goals. As you do, write down all the negative and resistant thoughts that come up.

When you sense yourself contracting, or the cells in your heart constricting, acknowledge the resistance you feel. And observe your thinking so you can become aware of the old, learned programming. What belief is holding you back from feeling the way you want to feel?

For each desire that you chose to focus on in the first exercise in this chapter (see page 60), detail the limiting voices you heard in your head. What did they say?

1._____

_____

_____

_____

_____

2._____

_____

_____

_____

_____

3._____

_____

_____

_____

_____

4._____

_____

_____

_____

_____

5._____

_____

_____

_____

_____

When limiting beliefs come up, it's important to acknowledge them, but not to agree with them. When I did this exercise, I found many limiting and constricting beliefs around money, such as:

- I must work hard and sacrifice for money.

- Wealthy people are not kind.

Your next step is to program your subconscious mind with new thoughts that serve you better. These thoughts will begin as affirmations. Repeating these affirmations will create new beliefs and program your **RAS** system to help you create a new reality.

My affirmations to undo my old programming about money were:

- Money flows easily to me.

- Money is the currency of gratitude; the more I have the more I can give.

As you work with affirmations that resonate with you, it will be imperative that you remember, not with just your head, but also with your heart, that with faith all things are possible. Whatever resistance you feel, whatever thought holds you back from stepping into all you desire, it needs to be disempowered, dismissed, and deleted from your belief system and replaced with a new belief that supports your highest self.

Now it's time to create affirmations of your own to work as antidotes to your current disempowering and limiting thought imprints. Some common subconscious imprints that hold people back are:

- "I am not worthy/deserving."

- "I need to earn love."

- "I am flawed."

- "I need to work hard and sacrifice for money."

- "My opinion doesn't matter."

- "I will be alone."

- "I am destined to fail."

Here are some examples of affirmations that you might want to use to help reprogram your mind.

- "I am always worthy of unconditional love."

- "I am whole, perfect, and complete."

- "I am the creator of everything in my life."

- "I deserve to be happy."

- "Money flows easily to me."

- "When I speak, people hear me. My voice has value, importance, and meaning."

- "I am infinite potential, so I can attract anything I want in my life."

- "I attract all that I need to serve my highest good."

Now design affirmations of your own that fully support each area of your life.

1._____

_____

_____

_____

2._____

_____

_____

_____

_____

3._____

_____

_____

_____

4._____

_____

_____

_____

5._____

_____

_____

_____

Using these empowering affirmations, you will be reprogramming your subconscious mind.

CHAPTER 5

Reprogram Your Mind with Meditation & Affirmations

YOU MAY BE WONDERING IF **it is possible to learn a new way of thinking? Yes, absolutely. You can reprogram your mind by combining meditation with deep, diaphragmatic breathing and affirmations. It only takes three weeks or so to build a neural pathway that can support and sustain a new belief system. This doesn't mean your negative old beliefs won't be triggered, but the sensations of resistance and constriction** in your body will be less impactful following your re-programming. Furthermore, your awareness of when you are in reaction rather than being motivated by your truth, will be heightened.

You can reprogram your mind by combining meditation with deep, diaphragmatic breathing and affirmations.

Let's demystify the whole idea of meditation. I think many people have preconceived notions of what the practice of meditating entails. You don't need to burn candles, sit on a pillow in the lotus position, or chant *om* to reap the benefits of meditation. Mind you, all the practices I've mentioned would likely support you in connecting with your highest self, but to begin to form the habit and enjoy the benefits of meditation, I encourage you to keep things simple.

Essentially, meditation is a conscious focus on the breath. As you sit and breathe deeply, you naturally quiet your thoughts. It is a simple but extraordinarily powerful way to help yourself create and feel inner harmony.

Sit or lay down in a location where you will not be disturbed. Assume a relaxed position, close your eyes, and breathe deeply into your belly while concentrating on the air filling your diaphragm. Sense the air moving in and out of your belly much like the tide of the ocean moving out and in.

I like to focus on all parts of my breathing because it busies my mind with breathing, which softens my focus on the other, crazy mental activity I've got going on. I place my hands on my belly. Then I feel for the cool temperature of the air being inhaled through my nose to a count of five, and feel my hand rising on my diaphragm as the air moves down into my lungs.

Once my lungs are full, I hold my breath for a second, and then I feel the warmth of the air as I exhale slowly to a count of five.

This breathing pattern—five counts in, one count held, and five counts out—allows for a full oxygen exchange. More oxygen enters the body and more carbon dioxide exits. It lowers the heart rate and the blood pressure by countering stress and the nervous system's fight-or-flight response. It reduces anxiety and muscle tension, and causes the body to release serotonin, a natural happiness hormone that can elevate your mood and give you a feeling of overall wellness.

There are many other benefits of diaphragmatic breathing, but to reprogram your subconscious brain, the one we care about most is that it puts you in a theta brain wave state, which is when you have access to your subconscious mind.

As you breathe, it is normal for thoughts to move through your mind. Don't judge or criticize yourself, simply softly acknowledge them and let them float out again. As your mind begins to still, and it will, you will access the state needed to reprogram your subconscious mind to create new beliefs that support your expansion.

After five minutes of breathing, repeat the affirmations you began working on in Chapter 4 aloud several times each, continuing for approximately five minutes.

After saying your affirmations, sit in silence and breathe naturally for five more minutes. You will feel the reprogramming throughout your entire body.

Just fifteen minutes per day of this practice of meditation and affirmations can change your life and the lives of others around you forever. I encourage you to embrace it as a morning ritual of:

- Five minutes of relaxation and breathing,

- Five minutes of saying affirmations and intentions with great feeling, and

- Five minutes of quiet stillness.

This fifteen minutes will heighten your focus, increase your energy, elevate your mood, enhance your productivity, and program your brain to go out all day long and prove new truths to you that will change your life from ordinary to extraordinary.

If you find fifteen minutes difficult, then set yourself up for success by starting with only five minutes. Do a minute of deep breathing, three minutes of affirmations and intentions, and one minute of stillness for relaxation and to build confidence.

"Now that I do affirmations, my life is in the best place it has ever been. I feel empowered and in total control of my destiny."

—JENN CONNON, AGE 34,
CUSTOMER SERVICE REPRESENTATIVE,
ENTREPRENEUR

After you do your meditation, celebrate your success. Observe the benefits and increase the amount of time you meditate as soon as you are ready to enhance the overall experience. If it's simply a matter of not thinking you have time to meditate, you might be mistaken.

I am telling you, we often don't know what we don't know. I firmly feel that if you want to transform your life you don't have time not to meditate!

New, much more empowering beliefs will start as affirmations. Through repetition, you will form a new neural pathway to experience a new reality, and you will be motivated to act and create with a new energy and attitudes that better serve you. That means you will close the gap between where you are now and where you want to be faster and more easily by meditating than you would do without. It's a good deal!

Remember, what gets scheduled gets done. Make your daily meditation an important appointment with yourself.

If you would like to listen to a variety of guided meditation audios, I invite you to visit my website, www.creatinglifebydesign.net, and receive several free downloads.

Remember, what gets scheduled gets done. Make daily meditation an important appointment with yourself.

CHAPTER 6

As You Think, So Shall You Be

NOW THAT YOU KNOW WHAT YOU WANT **to feel in each area of your life and you are building the neural pathways to believe that you can achieve it, it's time to set clear intentions.**

Setting an intention is different from having an expectation. This distinction is subtle, but important. Expectations often lead to resentment. Intentions open our minds to possibility. What's the difference? An expectation is something we hope another person will do. It is outwardly focused. An intention is an inwardly focused motivation that drives our own behaviour.

Expectations often lead to resentment.
Intentions open our minds to possibility.

Setting intentions will raise your vibration and help you to achieve your desired outcome, whereas expectations will lower your vibration, offer you fewer possibilities, and lead to frustration.

"My life has changed immensely. I have been given a new beginning because I state my intentions several times a day. I am open to all possibilities and ready for anything!"

—MARIA DEBROUWER, AGE 50,
CHILD AND YOUTH CARE WORKER

I recommend writing your intentions on paper. When writing your intentions, use your imagination to think about what outcome—when it has been achieved—will give you the full experience of all you wish to feel. Write down your hopes, desires, and wishes.

Remember, there are no limits! Now is not a time to set the bar so low that you cannot help but hit it. It's time to set the bar to match what your soul genuinely wants and dreams of for you. Setting a high bar for yourself will require you to suspend your disbelief and surrender control of exactly what the outcome will look like and how it will come to be. But I assure you that the way will be shown to you when you put the principles I am teaching you in this book into action.

It's time to set the bar to match what your soul genuinely wants and dreams of for you.

Perhaps one of your intentions is to see a certain amount of money deposited in your bank account each month. Your intention would look something like: "I AM a powerful entrepreneur bringing in $10,000 dollars or more month after month while sharing my passion for health and wellness."

You would say this instead of forming an expectation that is dependent on the behavior of other people, such as: "I AM promoted to the next level of management in my company where I now earn $10,000 per month."

A correctly worded intention always leaves multiple ways for the universe to align you with an outcome.

You could set intentions to find the business partner of your dreams, to achieve a certain level of health, or to establish a highly fulfilling relationship. Now it's time to put your order into the universe.

The tricky part for people is that they usually write intentions from the place where they currently live. They say things like: "I want a promotion and to have $10,000 coming in every month." *I want* doesn't work.

> You can't create what you desire through the thought process and energetic vibration of the lack of it.

Yes, you need to start by figuring out what you want, but that's not the end of the process of setting an intention. In truth, wanting is an idea of lacking. So, you can't *have* anything you *want—having* is an idea of abundance.

My point is that you can't create what you desire through the thought process and energetic vibration of the lack of it. The seeming paradox of manifesting what you want is probably the main reason why so many people don't live the lives they want to. They too often create from the energy of the wanting, rather than from the energy that aligns them with having their desires and goals fulfilled.

How do you prevent this? You must be in the frequency of already having the thing you desire in your reality. You need to act as though you already have it or are it. If you can dream it in your current imagination, you can make it your reality.

Albert Einstein, who amazed people with his innovation, said: "Imagination is more important than knowledge. For knowledge is limited to all we now know and understand, while imagination embraces the entire world, and all there will ever be to know and understand."

For me, voicing, even to myself, what I wished as if I was already living it, was a stumbling block because I have always prided myself on the fact that I was an honest person. I wanted to be a woman of my word. The problem was that my thoughts were in my current reality, so I continued to create more of my current reality.

Maybe you have heard the idea: "Fake it until you make it." This phrase made my skin crawl. But then I heard another phrase from my friend Thomas Tidlund that I liked better because it made everything click for me: "*Faith* it until you make it." I could do that. I had tremendous faith in my intentions. I knew they aligned with who I was as a person and with my unique talents and gifts. I could feel the joy in their creation. And I expressed this complete faith to myself in the privacy of my thoughts, affirmations, and intentions, until sure enough, when I implemented the rest of this process, doors opened, and creation happened with ease.

> I am the creator of my life and
> my life is meant to be extraordinary.

For others, it seemed almost like magic when I started making breakthroughs financially. But I now know my success was due to the science of inspired internal motivation. I was in vibrational alignment with my authentic desires. I simply took the limits off and realized that I am the creator of my life and my life is meant to be extraordinary.

As you play with the possibilities, create your intentions using the two most powerful words in the English dictionary: I AM. These words put you in the energy and the feeling of what you desire to create right now, and program your RAS to lead you to all you need to make that your reality.

I have carefully crafted affirmative I AM statements for all areas of my life. I say these with feeling during my morning meditation, on the stair-stepper, and in the grocery line (in my head). Just imagine how you will feel as you read these statements along with your clear intentions and you begin to know them as your truth.

- "I AM powerful."

- "I AM calm."

- "I AM strong."

- "I AM successful."

- "I AM confident."

- "I AM abundant."

- "I AM secure.,"

- "I AM unlimited."

- "I AM vital."

- "I AM creative."

- "I AM worthy."

- "I AM love."

Now it's time for you to write your own I AM statements. An intention should be phrased positively and in the present tense. When you say these statements, your body should feel great excitement and anticipation. If it doesn't, then you don't have the right statement; taking the time to reword it is imperative.

1.   I AM _____

_____

_____

_____

_____

2.   I AM _____

_____

_____

_____

_____

3.   I AM _____

_____

_____

_____

_____

4. I AM _____

_____

_____

_____

_____

5. I AM _____

_____

_____

_____

_____

When you set an intention, check in with yourself to be sure you are coming from a place of heart-centred desire with it. Ask yourself: Is this intention in alignment with my true self? Is this my authentic desire or is it someone else's expectation for me?

Is your intention a chance for you to express your best self, your passions, your unique talents and gifts to the world? It is in your best interest to create intentions that do not depend on anyone else. Be sure these are truly your intentions and do not need the same level of desire from another individual in order to achieve them.

Once you set the intention and you know it aligns with who you are at the core, you must relinquish any attachment you feel to that outcome. Instead of clutching at it, connect and live passionately in the energy of how you want to feel. The easiest way to amplify the energy of what you want to feel is to go back in your imagination to another time in your life where you felt that feeling before. Tapping into the feelings of that experience will help you to embody them.

For example, if you have the desire to feel great abundance, choice, and ease, think of other times in your life where you have felt those same feelings, and remember that energy frequency when you are speaking your intention. Perhaps you felt endless abundance, choice, and ease when you were on your last visit to an incredible food buffet. Remember how pleasing the choices in front of you were?

Feel into the endless number of dishes provided. Do you remember how as soon as a serving tray emptied someone came and filled it up again? Expand upon that feeling of continuous flow of abundance as you say your intention.

When you move through your life in the feeling of already having all you desire, your results become secondary. Frankly, you already feel so good from the process of creating a goal that you could take it or leave it, but feeling that good is the key to manifesting everything you desire.

Because intentional action comes from your true essence and deep internal inspiration to serve the world, you will find energy stores you never knew you had while you're working.

Setting intentions on their own does not guarantee success. Yes, it will increase the attraction of possibilities, people, and opportunities. But you must also take action with great clarity, energy, and grit. Because intentional action comes from your true essence and deep internal inspiration to serve the world, you will find energy stores you never knew you had while you're working. Doors will open to you with greater ease, but you must also lean in and walk through them.

The key is not to go back to being the human *doer* and get into the old, learned patterns of working hard doing things you *should do*. In fact, I encourage you to take the word *should* right out of your vocabulary. Don't try to micromanage the outcome.

Remember that the universe has a much broader view than you do of the possible ways to make your desired feelings become your reality. The art of surrender will help you to experience greater joy, ease, and flow in your life while you are waiting to learn more about those extraordinary pathways.

CHAPTER 7

Take Inspired,
Purposeful Action

ONCE YOU HAVE CLARITY ABOUT **your mission and have set a clear intention, the easiest way to figure out the next inspired action to take (which you need to do because you must take action) is to find someone who has accomplished something similar to what you want to achieve and learn from them. Get the road map, make a plan, learn the skills, build the competence, and then take incredibly focused action.**

Before you expend energy taking uneducated steps, recognize that success leaves clues. There is no need to take the long way to learning. Shorten your learning

curve by watching and modelling what has already
been proven to work.

With deep respect, learn from the best, but don't
hand over your power to external sources, such as clas-
ses, books, people, and so on, because the true power of
manifestation comes from you assimilating the information and then taking purposeful action imbued with
the energy of your self-expression.

If you chase too many dreams,
you won't achieve any.

You may have noticed that I did not ask you to create
twenty I AM statements in the last chapter. I want you
to weave the threads of your life into a well-rounded,
rich tapestry and keep your focus relatively narrow.
Having too many areas of focus simultaneously can
make you a jack of all trades and a master of none. If you
chase too many dreams, you won't achieve any.

These exercises were not set out in the order that
they were to make you think you could just "believe" or
meditate your dream life into existence. You must take
inspired, purposeful, consistent actions aimed directly
toward the creation of that which you desire, while to
the best of your ability, living in the energy of how you

will feel when you achieve them. Doing this takes focus, determination, and planning.

You need to become the king or queen of your calendar. Craft your days to create the life you desire. Your schedule is where the magic happens. When you plan, schedule at least three purposeful steps toward the achievement of each of your intentions every single day.

By putting these three steps toward each of your five intentions into your schedule and connecting these steps with the feelings you want to have, you have the recipe to achieve a reality that brings you great joy and inner harmony.

> You need to become the king
> or queen of your calendar.

You need to infuse these three actions toward a specific outcome with the feelings you intend to create. Therefore, they won't seem like huge, painful, time-consuming leaps toward accomplishing an outcome. These are just three small, intentional steps that are joyfully taking you directly toward your intended purpose.

I know three small actions may not seem like much on Day One, but the forward motion of making progress day after day creates momentum and can produce the result you desire faster than you imagine. Through consistent activity, by the end of one year you will have taken 1,095 steps to create your desired result. That can produce mind-blowing outcomes.

Imagine that one of your five intentions is to feel strong, lean, and filled with vitality. During the year, you take 1,095 steps, such as drinking more water, taking the stairs, cutting out one fast-food lunch, and similar actions. Can you see what the compound effect of those small choices would be after a year?

The tricky part is that these small, purposeful actions are easy to do, but also very easy *not* to do. That's where your commitment and grit need to be non-negotiable. Decide with a no-matter-what attitude that you will take the three action steps every single day.

Celebrate the little victories. Even years after I started using the ordinary to extraordinary formula, I still like to cross each step off my list to show that, yes, I have accomplished what I said I would do.

Creating a schedule of fifteen small action steps (3 steps x 5 intentions), may seem overwhelming at first, because you may not be accustomed to careful planning. But once it becomes a habit, it makes life less overwhelming. Crafting a life of focus, joy, and clear intentions feels good, which in turn produces big results.

Are you already coming up with excuses as to why you can't fit three small, purposeful actions toward one intention into your schedule every day? This issue is normal! It is a sign that your ego is trying to keep you where you are rather than allow you to move forward into new and uncharted territory.

You must remember, if you want something different, you must do something differently. Albert Einstein's famous quote often rings true for many of us with resistance to change: "The definition of insanity is doing the same thing over and over and expecting different results."

If you are struggling with how on earth you are going to fit three action steps into each of your already full days, you need to look closely at your schedule and master your time. Take all the "I shoulds" out of your calendar. When you *should* on yourself, you live your life for the happiness of others.

When you look at what in your schedule takes up your time right now, you may see how often you are doing things that are not taking you closer to leading the life you desire. Things like watching TV, mindlessly surfing for news of celebrities on the internet, or going to lunch with people you don't like very much can be replaced with intention-driven action steps. It's time to review your I AM statements. When the feelings you want to experience are fresh in your imagination, you will demand of yourself that you carve time out of every day for your action steps.

Time is your most precious resource. To live a life of inner harmony and to tap into your full potential, you must decide how best to spend your time. To become the master of your time, I encourage you to:

Step 1: Take everything that you *should do* or *have to do* off your calendar, and then ...

Step 2: For each item you removed, ask yourself: Do I still choose to do this?

Step 3: If you choose to do an item on your to-do list, find a way to infuse that task with some of the feelings you want to feel. You need to find a way to bring joy into everything you do. Otherwise, you'll resent how you spend your days and will attract more things you dis-like into your life.

Mindset is of absolute importance because it will de-termine the vibration of your energy field while com-pleting a task.

When I "have to" or "should" do something, I'm in a victim state with a low vibration and I will attract more of that feeling into my life.

Mindset determines your vibration.

When you choose to do something, you are in an em-powered state no matter what task you are completing. I choose to clean my toilets because I enjoy the feeling of coming into a clean bathroom, and because I feel em-barrassed when others come into my home and they are not clean. Even in this task, I'm choosing to move to-wards the clean bathroom and away from the dirty one, so I am motivated to take action.

I want to infuse the task of toilet cleaning with some of what I want to feel. I can feel more playful with higher energy when I crank some music while I clean the toilets, and I know that when the task is complete I will feel comfortable when I have people in my home using the bathrooms.

Changing your mindset will quickly increase your productivity and can even help make chores like cleaning fun.

Look at all the things that you choose to do, and ask yourself: By giving these choices time in my day, are they bringing me closer to the life I intend? Or am I doing them for reasons that have nothing to do with the life I want to live?

Give yourself permission to say no.

Seven years ago, when I looked at all the things that were eating up my time and yet not taking me closer to the life I wanted to create, I realized that I needed to start crafting my days differently. I gave myself permission to say no to the things that were not taking me towards my desires or allowing me to feel what I wanted to feel. Soon, I became comfortable saying no. This was very freeing.

At first, this kind of behaviour seemed selfish to me and others. The resistance I felt from others was uncomfortable because they could see me making different choices than I had previously. They were used to me just agreeing and adding another thing to my schedule.

Before I took control of my schedule, I derived my self-worth and personal validation from pleasing other people. I wasn't living my purpose. I wasn't pursuing my happiness. Developing awareness of my calendar was life changing for me. I realized I wanted and deserved something different. My true validation had to start to come from inside of me.

True validation comes from within.

I was determined to model a better, more authentic and joyful way of life for my children. When I started scheduling my days with three purposeful steps toward each of the five intentions I was working on at a particular time, I was able to present a different lifestyle to others. I became happier and was not nearly as frazzled by my schedule. I could be a better mother, friend, daughter, wife, teacher, and entrepreneur because I was living a self-expressed, authentic life.

Some things in our schedules are non-negotiable. These need to be blocked into your calendar first. Right now, for example, going to work to be able to pay your bills might be one of those non-negotiable items, one of the things you choose to do. Block your work time into your day and then find a way to surround that work with gratitude and whatever else you want to feel.

Even if your ultimate intention is to transition out of your current job, it is important to be focused and grateful for all you have right now. You can feel eager for the future while you are in the midst of creating other choices.

As you are blocking out all your non-negotiable tasks, ask yourself: Are all these things that are eating up my time truly non-negotiable? Then look for solutions that save you time. For instance, I can choose to pick up the kids from baseball or I can choose to form a car pool with other parents so I can use that same hour to take steps toward the intentions I want to achieve this year on the days when it's not my turn to do pickup.

Consider your options. Don't just automatically fall back on your old habits. Take control of your calendar and your life. Be the hero in your story, not the victim.

Time is the greatest way to leverage our efforts. We all have the same twenty-four hours in a day available to us. It's how we use those hours that makes us different. When you have all your chosen tasks blocked into your calendar, look at the time you have left. Start breaking down your intentions into small action steps, use the skills you have developed modelling those who have already done what you're trying to do, and then place those action steps into your schedule.

If creating the life you desire is important to you—meaning, if you have truly decided—you will find a way to make the time to perform these daily actions. Ultimately, you won't go to bed until you have done them.

If you are making excuses for why you can't fit those steps into your day, then you also need to take responsibility for the path you have chosen—because you are the creator of your life and your life is made up of your days, your hours, and your minutes.

Often fear lies behind an excuse not to take action. So, I'm going to ask you to take a deep breath and remember that the fears you have in your head sometimes are not your truth. Find the old subconscious imprint, the learned belief that no longer serves you, use an affirmation—a truth that your adult person knows—and then lean in and take the steps you need to take anyway.

One technique I use to help me be more productive and get the most out of my hours is to schedule the hard stuff first. When you accomplish the hard stuff first, it builds your confidence, strength, power, and clarity.

Until you do the hard stuff, distractions will clutter your brain. Often when I have the hard stuff done first thing in the morning, I can't help taking a few more steps toward my intentions because I have created momentum.

I review my I AM statements and take the time to schedule my next day's activities at night before bed. That way, I'm fully prepared to get the most out of my days right from the get-go every morning. When you look at the patterns of many successful people, you will notice that a tremendous number of them get up early.

I can almost hear the groans from many of my readers now. I know rising early is not for everyone, but if you are looking for a way to add more time and productivity into your days, rising an hour earlier is a respectable option. Speaking for myself, I am most productive when I get up early. Among other things, this gives me time to make a gratitude list. I want to start my day in a state of being grateful for what I already have. When you are grateful, the universe often gives you more for which to be grateful.

After making my gratitude list, I do my meditation with the diaphragmatic breathing, affirmations, and feeling into my intentions.

Then I wash up, down a ton of water to beat the dehydration from the night, and I read or watch something inspiring to put my mind in a positive place.

Next, I do a short cardio/body resistance workout.

After those few actions, I'm already set up to have a most productive day.

If you think that this sounds like something you would like to do, but you need help to create this habit, I invite you to visit www.CreatingLifeBydesign.Net and join my free challenge, *30 Days to a New Morning Habit and a Happier Healthier You.* You get up at your desired time, wash up, drink some water, and click to watch a fifteen-minute video on your computer, tablet, or smartphone. I serve as your accountability partner and coach. Each day, in the video, I offer a positive mindset tip and then lead a twelve-minute high- intensity interval training (HIIT) workout with modifications offered for all levels of fitness that will have you sweating, toned, and productive for the rest of the day.

"My husband and I have been implementing the ordinary to extraordinary formula. Not only has it changed both of us positively but now our children are learning by example how to stay positive, be grateful, and be the best versions of themselves. Things in our household have changed dramatically!"

—CARLY MOORE, AGE 34,
HAIRSTYLIST AND ENTREPRENEUR

It took practice for me to get good at scheduling my days to create the life I desire. I created habits that aligned with the life I wanted and how I wanted to feel. Then I practiced with commitment. Yes, there were days that weren't perfect, but I learned to have compassion for myself and come back to the moment and commit myself again.

Life is about progression, not perfection. As I reflect on where I am, it has served me to soften my self-criticism and learn to live from a place in which I know that the decisions I'm making will allow me to be better tomorrow than I was today. You are meant to live an amazing life filled with all the best our human existence has to offer. Creating habits and carving out the time to take purposeful action not only will bring you joy, but it will also produce incredible results over time. You deserve them.

Life is about progression, not perfection.
Be better today than you were yesterday.

Be Ready, Allow, & Experience the Wonder

IF YOU HAVE GONE THROUGH THE STEPS **in this book so far, you are on the right path to go from ordinary to extraordinary. Absolutely! You only need to have:**

- **Taken inventory of the areas of your life that lack potential.**

- **Identified the gifts learned from your lessons up to this point.**

- **Chosen how you would like to feel and realized you are worthy of those feelings.**

- Set clear intentions to manifest what you desire.

- Done what was necessary to learn the skills involved in your dream and taken consistent, purposeful action.

Like a farmer, you have cultivated the soil and planted high-quality seeds. Now simply enjoy watering and fertilizing your crops and have the faith that the harvest will be even greater than your imagination has predicted. You can do this with patience and trust if you are living in the energy and joy of already having it.

This time of allowing is where the real magic happens. It is a time when you need to acknowledge and honour that you are a human being (not a human doing). When you have put the rest of the plan into action, you must take the time to breathe and trust that you, just being, are enough.

When you think of the most powerful moments in a stage play or the most poignant evoking moments in music, it's when the piece of art is in momentum and then we have silence. The magic in the music happens between the notes. The most powerful times on stage are when an actor chooses silence.

Silence also is your time to settle in and give the universe the grace and space to provide the next right opportunity. When you incorporate this new way of living into your approach, the result becomes an appreciated albeit unnecessary byproduct because the joy of the journey is so great. That, my friend, is a life well lived. That is living fully in the present with huge joy and appreciation and yet an eager excitement, much like an anticipatory child on Christmas morning.

"Tabatha teachings are powerful yet gentle and have helped me to find new ways of sharing my joy in creatively expressing the experience of life through art with others."

—CHRISTINE REILLY CARTER, AGE 65,
ARTIST AND BUSINESS OWNER

You want to stay in this energy as much as possible, and when you do, you will see things unfold for you that you could never have predicted. You will live in a state of wonder and amazement of how things are happening for you. You will begin seeing new creative opportunities arise around you.

But we're human, so of course, our egos are going to try to create doubt and use every trick they can to prove to you that it's not worth it and you are going to fail. When we don't have proof of the results as quickly as we want, the human tendency is to want to go dig up the seeds we've planted to see if they are growing. Remember that you will never have a crop if you don't allow your plants to grow and their fruit to mature in its own perfect time. When doubt emerges, we often look around at others, and their success and make comparisons. Comparison can rob us of our joy of the journey.

Live in a state of wonder and amazement at how things happen for you.

I am only telling you about the hazards of comparison because you need to know the pitfalls so you can anticipate them and be prepared. When this happens, you want to be unwavering in speaking your affirmations and with your intention practices.

When you feel the energy of doubt or skepticism moving through you, stay away from social media. We have access to everybody's life at the click of a button these days, but when you are in a low vibration and surf social networks you will be tempted to compare your worst moments to everyone else's highlight reel.

Making a comparison is not going to support your energy vibration or your intention. In fact, it will likely suck you into negative, self-sabotaging loop that gains momentum. Use the tools in Chapter 3 to help you move up the vibrational scale.

Another common snag most people experience when beginning to live up to their full potential is negativity from the people with whom they are closest. It is important to be aware that when you act to create something different in your life, those around you are likely to feel uncomfortable. Sometimes, they are fearful because they love you and don't want to see you floundering around in unknown territory.

The ego of some of your friends and family members may feel threatened. Sometimes taking deliberate action to better your life shines a big spotlight on the fact that they are not doing the same. What happens if you grow and change? Will they be left behind? They may not be aware of why they are reacting the way they are, or be willing to admit to it, as their subconscious imprints are motivating them. But in reaction to your progress, they may start sending out messages of resistance.

Sometimes those messages can be loud and other times painfully silent. Either way, because you want these people to support you, understand you, and be excited for you, their resistance can throw you for a loop.

Remember, having expectations of others can lead to resentment. Love people where they are, set boundaries if needed, and give them a show they can't ignore.

The fact is that you can't control what people do or say, you can only control how you respond to them. Always be respectful, but hold your power.

Are you familiar with the crabs in a bucket analogy? When one crab tries to climb out, the others are determined to keep pulling it back down. Give people grace, keep your emotionally charged desire in front of you, and keep climbing your "bucket walls." Confidence is like a muscle: With work, it can grow and strengthen.

As you continue to live your life authentically and with full self-expression, you will give permission to others to do the same. Dimming your light to make others feel comfortable around you does not serve them or the rest of humanity. Hold onto your power and stay on your path to fulfill your potential, as it is the greatest gift you can share with the world.

Marianne Williamson explains this beautifully in this passage from her book *A Return to Love.*

Our deepest fear is not that we are inadequate. Our deepest fear is that we are powerful beyond measure. It is our light, not our darkness, that most frightens us. We ask ourselves, Who am I to be brilliant, gorgeous, talented, fabulous? Actually, who are you not to be? You are a child of God. Your playing small does not serve the world. There is nothing enlightened about shrinking so that other people won't feel insecure around you. We were born to make manifest the glory of God that is within us. It is not just in some of us; it's in everyone. And as we let our own light shine, we unconsciously give other people permission to do the same. As we are liberated from our own fear, our presence automatically liberates others.

Confidence is like a muscle: With work, it can grow and strengthen.

CHAPTER 9

The Ego Gets Clever

AS YOU CONTINUE FURTHER DOWN **your path of self-discovery and creation, you may notice a few things. Perhaps you are making nice, incremental progress towards your goals and you desire more radical transformation. If this is the case, you need to assess whether you have some subconscious imprints holding you back from ease and rapid expansion. It could be a subconscious thought you simply had not noticed before, such as:**

- **"Achieving success is a difficult path."**

- **"Anything worth doing takes time."**

- "I'm not supposed to be more successful than my parents."

Reprogramming the subconscious brain is like peeling an onion, there is always another layer. My point is that you must continue to look for the areas of your thinking that are still limiting you.

You may have noticed that your ego is no longer showing you a fear of failure. You have shifted to believing that you are worthy and capable and the creator of everything you desire in your life. Then, one day, your ego might turn up the heat and show you a new set of deeply rooted subconscious beliefs related to a fear of success.

Achieving your desires always puts you in unexplored territory.

Having inner resistance heat up as you make progress is normal because achieving your desires always puts you in unexplored territory. Every time you go out of your comfort zone, your sense of identity will feel threatened. That's the ego at work.

You could fall into the trap of feeling that now you have more to lose. The stakes are higher so there is more at risk. Your ego could tell you something dismaying like: "The higher you climb, the farther you have to fall." All these types of beliefs are learned beliefs that cause us to contract and pull back.

To overcome this type of thinking, simply go back and apply the steps in Chapter 4. We are always works in progress. Life is not about arriving at a destination; it's a journey of self-discovery. So, celebrate your awareness of your limiting beliefs each time a new one crops up, recognize that it was learned and no longer serves you. Thank it say, "I appreciate the help, but I've got this."

Life is a journey of self-discovery.

Create new affirmations from the point of view of your adult self, so you can disempower the beliefs you learned as a child. When you use these powerful affirmations consistently and with feeling in meditation, you create new beliefs and neural pathways that support your continued progress. Be kind to yourself on this journey as you are learning to let more love and abundance into your life.

Maybe you are in flow and you are consistently unlocking your potential and massive success is moving freely into your life. I'm thrilled for you! But I do want to make you aware of another trick the ego can start playing, which is the trick of making you feel like you are better than others. Smarter, faster, luckier, better. When you are at the top of your game your ego can motivate you to judge and alienate the people around you.

All you ever need to do in any given moment is be the best you that you can be and allow other people to be the best them they can be.

The people you are judging may not be privy to the knowledge that they are the creators of everything in their lives. They may not be aware that they embody infinite potential. If your confidence becomes arrogance, you will flip into a low vibration that is not truth, but a learned belief. This is a difficult belief to dissolve because society fosters a got-to-be-the-best mentality.

From experience, I believe that healthy competition is incredibly motivating, but not when people's self-worth is attached to the outcome. Not when another human being must be labelled as less than you or is felt to be less than you for you to succeed or feel successful. If you feel that you need to be the best all the time, you will never feel true inner harmony. And people won't like being around you.

A key ingredient of success is to remember that we are all on a path that is unfolding perfectly. One human is not superior than another. All you ever need to do in any given moment is be the best you that you can be, and allow other people to be the best them that they can be. No one needs to be fixed.

When we turn to judging people, we must remember that we are judging ourselves equally harshly. What we see in others is always mirroring something for us. Therefore, practice speaking to everyone you interact with using the same level of kindness and respect you wish to be returned.

Have you encountered someone you would characterize as extremely successful only to find out that they're not happy or that they're hard on themselves and others? If so, it is because they are still creating from a place of lack and not enoughness. You don't want to fall into this way of life.

It is important to continue to expand your self-love and serve the world from a place that is infinite. As you progress, this means you become capable of sharing more love and more acceptance, so you can uplift and inspire others to step into their own greatness. The more you see the light in others, the more you will acknowledge and expand the light within yourself.

As you continue to grow, you will notice that people come and go from your life. As your energy vibration changes, you will repel some people and you will attract others. This can be a trigger to go back to old patterns of thought and behaviour. It can suck some people back into a life of unfulfilled potential.

To hold steady in your progress, simply realize that some people come into your life for a reason, some for a season, and some for a lifetime. Isn't that beautiful? It's so accepting of reality.

"One of the greatest lessons I've taken from Tabatha's teaching is that change starts with me. Taking time to fill my own cup by eating well, exercising, and looking inward has significantly impacted how I feel, think, and interact with others personally and professionally. I am more balanced and confident."

—NIKKI BOWMAN, AGE 31, ENTREPRENEUR

When you are living in your flow, you won't manipulate people or try to make a reason a season, or a season a lifetime, which is why it is of the utmost importance to be sure you love yourself so much that you can give to others from your abundance rather than look to them to complete you. A healthy relationship between two people is one where both people are so good within themselves that they simply add to the other, rather than needing that other to compensate for the lack they feel.

If you need another person to provide your happiness, you are basically giving all your power away whether they want it or not.

Never forget that you are responsible for your own happiness. If you're happy you can offer your best freely to others rather than ask or need something from them.

It is of the utmost importance to be sure you love yourself so much that you can give to others from your abundance rather than look to them to complete you.

Being aware of common points of deterrence on the path to achieving your intentions can help you nip problems in the bud as they arise. Setbacks are normal. They are not failures, but important steps in your journey of self-discovery. When new imprints arise, simply go back to the chapter that provides the tools for your positive expansion.

CHAPTER 10

What's Next?

YOU MAY BE EXPERIENCING THE FEELING **of
Now what? If you have set clear intentions and programmed your brain to help you implement the actions
to achieve them, you may have reached the top of the
mountain you were climbing. If so, take time to celebrate and feel appreciation. Then, lift your chin and
look for the next mountain peak.**

**Before you move on to your next adventure, be sure
to take inventory of how far you've come, all you've
learned, how much you've grown, and the areas of your
life that bring you the greatest joy. You'll know these
areas because when you're spending your time with
them you're doing great things, time flies by, your soul
is on fire, and you're making a difference.**

"With pure passion and profound simplicity, Tabatha's tools have inspired me to dream bigger and reminded me that I can and will make an impact."
—KIM WIDEMAN, AGE 48, ENTREPRENEUR

Start playing with the possibilities again. Put pen to paper and ask yourself to complete the sentence: *WHAT IF?* Teach yourself the skill of dreaming even bigger. This is how your joyful life can continue to expand, and it is also how world advancement happens. Everything starts with an idea.

At one time, The Wright Brothers wondered, *WHAT IF we could invent, build, and fly the world's first airplane?*

Martin Luther King, Jr., wondered, *WHAT IF I could help end racism?*

Oprah Winfrey may have wondered, *WHAT IF I could become one of the most positively influential people in the world?*

How would you finish the sentence, *WHAT IF?*

You now know you are the creator of everything in your life, someone filled with infinite possibility. It's time to realize new desires.

Don't overthink this exercise. Just ask yourself, **WHAT IF . . . ?** and then write down the first ten ideas that come to mind.

What if _____

_____ ?

What if _____

_____ ?

What if _____

_____ ?

What if _____

_____ ?

What if _____

_____ ?

What if _____

_____ ?

What if _____

_____?

What if _____

_____?

What if _____

_____?

What if _____

_____?

Now read over the list you just made and put a star next to the ideas that make your cells expand with excitement.

Then, go back to Chapter 1 and start the process over again, bringing to it all the spectacular knowledge you gained the last time you went through it.

"Limitations live only in our minds.
But if we use our imaginations,
our possibilities become limitless"
—JAMIE PAOLINETTI

The Ripple Effect of Your Self-Expression Is Limitless

I AM TRULY GRATEFUL FOR **the time and attention you have dedicated to reading this book. It brings me great joy to share this information and my story with others, so that they can take from it what serves their higher purpose. Whether you read all the chapters in one sitting or several sittings doesn't matter; I hope you now feel equipped with a new level of awareness, high motivation, and a powerful set of tools to implement. I** can't wait for you to experience your magic-carpet-ride life and for you to be the mirror for others' growth.

If you stopped and actively did the exercises, it is my sincere hope that you are discovering how freak'n' amazing you are. My wish for you is that you fall madly in love with your far from perfect self and stand in your powerful self-expression, experiencing joy and adventures that were far beyond your imagination when you first opened the book. I would love to hear from you with details of how your life has gone from ordinary to extraordinary by working with this ten-step process. And then returning to the beginning, setting new goals, and making more strides to achieve your dreams.

Feel free to share your story with me via the Creating Life By Design Facebook page or by posting a comment on www.CreatingLifeByDesign.net.

Please pass this information and these tools forward to others to help raise the world's level of consciousness and unconditional love.

Thank you for having the courage and discipline to stand in your light. Together, we can light the way for many others. *Namaste.*

Resources

VISIT WWW.CREATINGLIFEBYDESIGN.NET **and gain access to additional resources specifically designed to help you reprogram your approach to life and unlock inspired success beyond your wildest imagination. Let us help you achieve your best self.**

Through CreatingLifeByDesign.net, contact us or connect with us on social media to stay up to date on the latest news, features, updates and inspiration.

THE BEST IN ME HONOURS THE BEST IN YOU

ABOUT THE AUTHOR

TABATHA DEBRUYN **is an inner harmony expert, a success coach, a motivational speaker, and a field leader and executive national vice president with a leading health and wellness social marketing company. In her private practice, her passion is to teach others to tap into their infinite potential and stand confidently and joyfully in the power of their true self-expression. As a mom of two teenage boys, a former high school teacher, and a trainer for thousands of startup entrepreneurs, she has extensive experience in helping people transcend fear and step into their power. Tabatha's training specializes in subconscious programming, and she is currently a doctoral candidate in metaphysical psychology at the University of Metaphysics and University of Sedona. You can access her free guided meditation series and *30 Days to a Happier, Healthier You* program at www.CreatingLifeByDesign.net.**